CHESTER

The Iridescent Dragonfly

By Gail Easling
Illustrated by Vencho

CHESTER: THE IRIDESCENT DRAGONFLY

Printed in the United States of America

ISBN 978-1-5399-9086-4

Gail Easling
P.O. Box 317
Winona, TX 75792

Illustrations copyright © 2016 by Vencho, www.fiverr.com/vencho
Book design by Sunlight Desktop Publishing, www.SunlightDTP.com

This book is dedicated to our sweet grandchildren,
especially Benjamin, Riley, and Peyton,
who are currently living a life of adventure on the great plains.

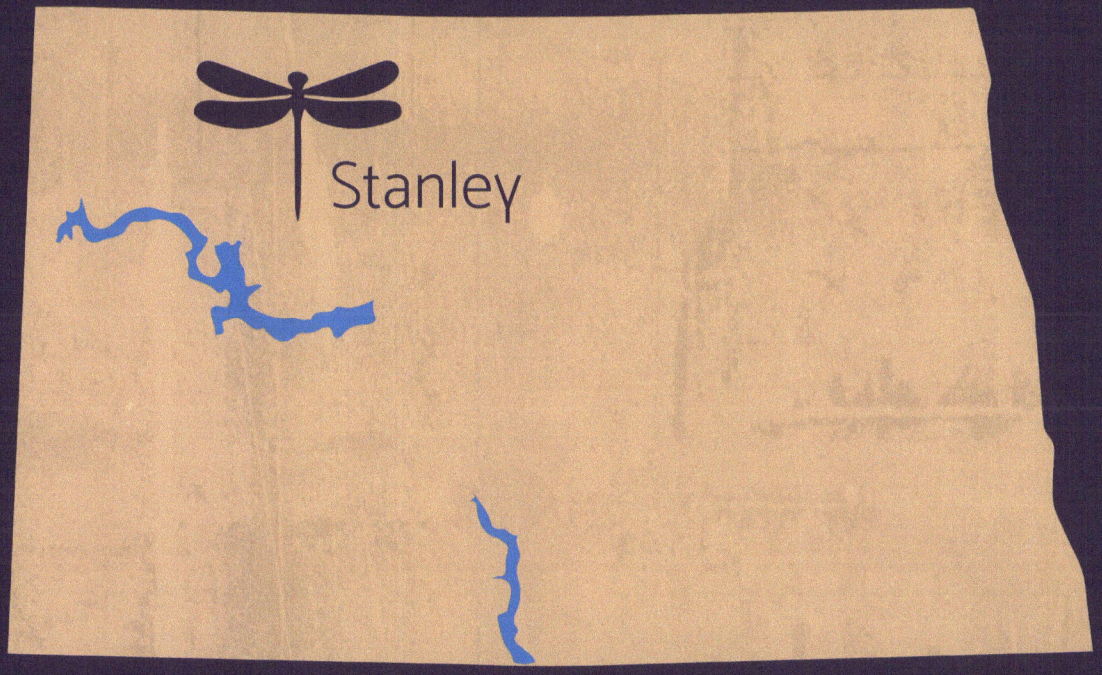

Stanley

North Dakota

The morning sun rose above the
grassy fields of North Dakota.

The chilly blanket of fog above the pond
was warmed by the cheerful rays of sunlight.

Hidden away in a little farm house,
nestled in the grasses of the great plains,
were three delightful children,
snuggly tucked away in their cozy beds.

Every day they looked forward to new adventures.

Today they were going to meet Chester,
the iridescent dragonfly.

For months, Chester had been living
in the pond near their home.

They hadn't noticed him,
because he looked very different then.

He had been a nymph.
He had made his home in the water
at the edge of the pond.

He ate mosquito eggs.

But today Chester is a new creation.
His old life is left behind.
Beneath him lay his old body.
Everything has changed.

His long slender body and beautiful glowing wings
sparkled in the sunlight.

As he sat in the morning sun, drying his wings,
he could feel his wings growing strong,
and he felt a new sense of power and freedom.

Encouraged by the brightness of the rising sun
he decided to try out his glistening wings.

Flying into the bright blue sky, he was delighted to see how quickly he could move.

He discovered he could move effortlessly, darting about in a free flowing dance.

As the sun rays filled the sky,
Chester saw his body gleaming in the sunlight.

Brilliant colors dazzled his eyes.

He could see farther
than he had ever seen before.
He looked back at the little pond
that had been his home.
He thought about the fog that
had covered his world.

He was no longer limited
by the life he left behind.
Chester was free.

Darting, dashing, hovering, dancing.

It wasn't long before he discovered
he was not alone.

The sky was full of
other joyful dragonflies
who were radiant and sparkling
in the morning sun.

They admired each other's
glistening bodies and bright colors.
They were grateful to be free.

All morning long they played together,
chasing mosquitoes.

As the morning light grew brighter, Chester noticed three children running toward them.

The tall grasses of the countryside had hidden them from sight.

Now the air was filled with their excited voices and joyful laughter.

All afternoon, the children
chased Chester and his little friends.

The dragonflies soared high in the sky
then returned again,
darting and dashing above their heads.

It wasn't long before the sun began to set.

A voice from the distant farm house
called for the children to come home.

As the children's silhouettes
disappeared across the grassy plain,
the light of day faded away.

Chester was grateful for
a day in the warm summer sun.
Chester was glad to be free.

Fun Dragonfly Crafts

Now it's your turn to be creative and have some fun. Craft dragonflies of your own. Let your imagination and creativity express themselves. Go outside and find sticks, maple seeds, driftwood, and shells. Or find shimmering paint, pipe cleaners, or buttons. See what you can do to create Chester and his friends. Have a joy filled day.

Author's Note

First, I want to thank you for purchasing this book. Lord willing, there will be many more to come.

It is my desire to give to the world a sense of God's great wonder. He is a magnificent creator! There is a whole world for us to discover along with our children, to thank Him for, and to learn from. May you find many more stories to delight you and your family, stories that will become a foundation and legacy for generations to come.

Tips for Parents & Teachers

Creating a sense of wonder is at your fingertips. All around you are opportunities to engage your children in the lessons of life.

In the story of Chester, there are many such hidden lessons.

First and foremost is the story of salvation. Jesus' death on the cross allows us to live in the power of His greatness. His sacrificial death for our sins has made it possible to be born again and find the freedom that He purchased.

Like Chester, we can have new life. Because of Jesus' sacrifice, we can receive the gift of salvation through His shed blood. The fog of the world (our sin and temporal values) keeps us earthbound, not being able to see far beyond our present situations and circumstances. When the brightness of His word (the Bible) and the voice of His Holy Spirit begin to shine His light into our lives, we gain a new and living perspective. We begin to see life from a whole new and bigger vantage point.

Another discovery is that Jesus has called and created many others, who are also free. Together, each one of us brings a bright radiance of God's glory and grace. The attacks of our enemy and our limiting beliefs (those pesky mosquitoes and the skins that bind us) can be overcome and shed. We can break free.

When you read this story with children, help them notice the changes in the illustrations. The illustrator, Vencho, has created pages that have similarities and differences. Explore the pictures with the children and see if they can spot what is the same and what is different. Enjoy the search.

It is my prayer that you seek God with all of your heart and soul and strength and mind, until you find Him and are set free.

Glossary

Agile means quick and well-coordinated in movement, nimble. Active, lively. It is the ability to think and move quickly.

Glistening means to reflect a sparkling light or a faint intermittent glow, as a sleek or wet surface; to shine lustrously. To sparkle.

Iridescent is displaying a play of lustrous changing colors like those of the rainbow.

Nymph is the young of an insect that undergoes incomplete metamorphosis or change.

Silhouettes are a two-dimensional representation of the outline of an object, as a person's profile, filled in with black.

There is great value in introducing children to new words. Building their vocabulary heightens their thinking processes and strengthens their minds to grow in wisdom and understanding. Create in them the capacity to learn and grow.

Definitions adapted from *Random House Webster's College Dictionary.*

About the Author

Gail Easling is an ordinary person who believes in an extraordinary God.

It is because of His greatness that she lives and moves and has her being.

In the ordinary, everyday world, God proves to be all He claims to be. He has shown Himself to be the provider of all of her family's needs. He is the great I AM.

As the years have come and gone, the great and mighty God of the universe has proven to be her family's provider, the giver of every good and perfect gift, the one who sanctifies our lives, redeems us from our sin, heals us, and is more than anything that we can ask or think or even imagine.

In the midst of an evil and corrupt culture and world, God has been her sustainer, deliverer, and the glory and the lifter of her head.

It is to Him she owes her life and her existence. In the midst of her loneliness He loved her. He healed her broken heart, and He set at liberty her soul and spirit that had been bound in the lies of the enemy.

To Him be all glory and praise.

www.ingramcontent.com/pod-product-compliance
Lightning Source LLC
Chambersburg PA
CBHW041529280526
45792CB00004B/1427